This is a

© Carolyn Emerick 2018

Illustration from "Christmas Sunshine" published in 1913 by the Hayes Lithographing Co

2

Table of Contents

1	The Northern European Folk-Soul Rooted in Our Holiday Traditions	4
2	The Hidden History of Christmas Carols	31
3	Christmas in Olde Wales	48
4	Christmas Carols & Customs	63
5	The Lost Female Figures of Christmas	82
6	The Yuletide Spirit: Heartbeat of our Folk-Soul	106

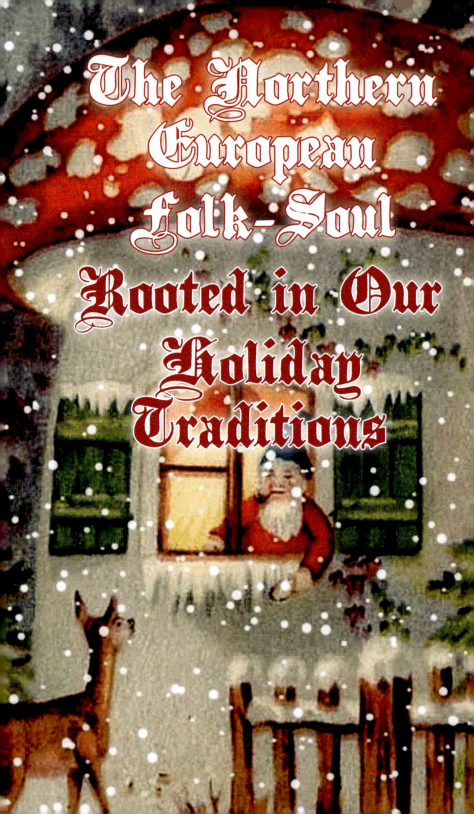

Chapter Contents

History's Tendency to be Elusive	6
Different Sources for Ascertaining History	8
The Mytho-Linguistic Key	10
Lazy Historians and the Filter of Bias	13
Congruence and Continuity	17
The Easter Controversy	20
What is the European Folk-Soul?	25
Our Folk-Soul is Our Salvation	27
Bibliography and Further Reading	30

History's Tendency To Be Elusive

Over the past several years I have researched several European holidays as part of a deeper cultural study of folk belief, and I have found that very often the "history" told on networks like "The History Channel" tends to be quite lazy. It was researching origins of folk customs and beliefs in general that has rendered me of the opinion that history is a very murky thing, indeed. A historian is trained that it is incorrect to claim the veracity of a thing without some kind of hard evidence. The problem is, in many cases the evidence has been lost to the mists of time. Now, any lawyer will tell you that absence of evidence is not evidence of absence. But, somehow this truth gets lost on too many historians who will overextend their authority to declare origins of a practice based on the earliest example of "evidence," or claim a thing never existed because there is no hard evidence for it. However, this years-long study has also shown me that there are other forms of evidence that historians have been slow on the uptake to consider, such as linguistics and folklore.

Finding roots of our holiday customs is complicated because so many of our holiday traditions have origins that began when Europeans were still practicing their indigenous faith – back when mythos, language, culture, and ethnicity were all one and the same thing; a holistic whole. But, when the ruling classes adopted Christianity

culture, and so stories, beliefs, myths, legends, genealogies, and historical accounts were passed down orally. Christian purge campaigns not only engaged in destroying what written works there were, but there are numerous historical accounts of massive purges of the wise people who held this knowledge; both at the point of conversion and much later during the next great political religious upheaval – the Protestant Reformation.

It is my view that real and true understanding of the past, and especially the beliefs of the people of the past (as opposed to a timeline of events and facts), can only be a multi-disciplinary approach. Looking solely at documentary evidence means we are buying into the version of history that the elite wanted passed down to posterity – a heavily biased lens which is essentially propaganda.

We can certainly look at archaeology and that can inform us on material culture, which can tell us how people lived. Archaeology can somewhat inform us to people's beliefs because by their possessions and structures we can start to learn what they valued. But, imagine if someone 500 years into the future found a teenage girl's bedroom from the 1950s filled with Elvis Presley records and posters on her wall. The archaeologist could see that Elvis Presley was an important figure, but without context, all manner of interpretations could be put on this "evidence." It could well be interpreted that Elvis was a god who had a large cult of devotion among young women in 20th century American society. Without context, material evidence is very much a best guess scenario.

them. Certain deities' importance to a tribe can be verified by the name of a town, hill, river, rock formation, or what have you, that was named by the local tribe who venerated that deity.

When we understand the myths of the past and the trails of language, the folk tradition can burst into life with added dimensions that would be missed by those without the contextual information. Customs, sayings, motifs, archetypes, and other elements will begin to pop out of our folklore. For example, in my Fairy Tales Series I was able identify a vestigial memory of the Teutonic mythic figures called the Norns, which are the Germanic equivalent to the Greek Fates, due to both symbolic imagery associated with them and the words they used. Not knowing the symbols associated with the Norns and not knowing the etymology of the words used in the tale would have let these figures pass right over the head of the reader without recognition. So this is one type of "evidence" that historians are typically not looking for, and not trained to recognize.

In other words, a historian looking at the documentary record will cite the point of conversion of a country by the date recorded in the historical chronicle which was written by a monk or church cleric, or an appointee of the monarch who commissioned the writing. In almost all cases, the monarchs converted for political reasons. Therefore there was a vested interest to declare they ruled a Christian country for the sake of alliances with other Christian monarchs united under the Pope. But, without bothering to look at the folk tradition, without a background in the mythos of that culture, and without certain linguistically etymological understandings, they would completely miss profound evidence that European Native Faith was alive and well all along!

For all of these reasons, looking to our oral histories passed down through the folk tradition is paramount to getting to the crux of cultural questions that we simply do not have other kinds of evidence for. The problem is that historians in general tend not to look toward these sources. One wonderful example is how the Norse sagas had been dismissed as legendary for so many years, but in recent years many accounts of the Viking explorers' exploits have been verified by some other means; such as archaeology or other corroborating evidence.

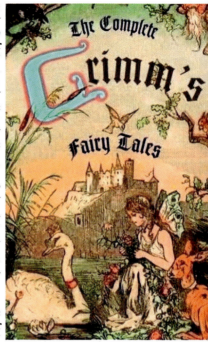

Returning to the folktale featuring the Norns, if we were to believe the documentary history, then we should think that England was fully Christian by the early Middle Ages. But, the said folktale (The Three Heads of the Well) demonstrates that the ancient mythos of the Anglo-Saxons was alive and well in the folk consciousness well into the Modern Era. And this same phenomena is especially prevalent in our holiday lore and imagery. Figures, symbols, and motifs that define our modern holidays are demonstrations of how strongly the beliefs of our very ancient ancestors have thrived and lived on in the European cultural consciousness even when we were not fully aware of it.

Lazy Historians and the Filter of Bias

Because the Christianization of Northern Europe was also essentially a Mediterranean cultural colonization and acculturation, the new Christian order brought with it Mediterranean practices and focus. So while the proliferation of writing is generally seen as a positive development, essentially the writing was all being done by a minority elite (monks, Church clerics) who held a deep seeded bias toward a Mediterranean Christian worldview. Indeed, they wrote in Latin, not in the native languages of Northern Europe. And they did so with the Roman alphabet while local alphabets were suppressed (this is a little different in the case of the Slavs, but that is a long tangent). Therefore, when historians, especially the lazy historians on the History Channel, look at history to find origins of certain customs, they will find the records kept by the Church and, in many cases due to personal religious bias on the part of more recent historians themselves, they will announce that a practice has a Christian origin because they can find no earlier record of it preceding the Church writings.

I found this to be the case when I researched an article called "The Hidden History of Christmas Carols." Lazy history would have you believe that the practice has a

Christian origin because hard evidence before 14th century is very difficult to pin down. Due to previous research I had done on the old holiday of Candlemas (now mostly forgotten), I knew that the custom of caroling had to have had a pre-Christian origin. A scholar by the name of Trefor M. Owen discusses caroling being done at Candlemas in old Wales in his article "The Celebration of Candlemas in Wales" published in Folklore Journal. It turns out that going door to door at holidays was a regular thing not only in Britain, but widespread in Europe, and not only at Christmas but throughout the year.

Pinning down the origins of a custom can often take deductive reasoning and analytic examination due to the reasons outlined above. Lazy historians will look at the Church re-packaged view of Christmas caroling (keeping with the same example) and, because it reinforces the heavy Christian bias that was inherent in Western academia before this current epoch (which has flipped to an equally strong bias in the opposite direction of secular atheism, and I oppose both), researchers will essentially abandon their search at the point where the Church re-packaged the custom. But, if you go further back, one can find that Church edicts and letters exist wherein a slightly different form of caroling is admonished.

Looking at the Church records, we can see that caroling was being opposed by the Roman Catholic Church from the time of its very earliest presence in Northern Europe. Sandra M. Salla is a contributor to a fantastic resource called Medieval Folklore, an encyclopedia of folkloric terms. In her entry for "Carols," Salla says that "between 600 and 1500 C.E. the Church formally banned the dancing of carols on church grounds" and that numerous informal "decrees, sermons, and exempla were written condemning the activity" (Salla, p61). Well, in 600 A.D., Britain was only newly nominally converted and pagan customs were still common among the peasantry. That the Church condemned this practice demonstrates that it was seen as pagan and they were attempting to stomp it out. Like many native European customs, the practice was so embedded in the consciousness of the people, eventually an "if you can't beat 'em, join 'em" approach was taken.

Another bit of corroborating circumstantial evidence for native European origins of Christmas caroling as opposed to a Christian one is that it is an example of "visiting customs," that is the tradition of going door to door throughout the village at a holiday, and this practice is firmly rooted in Heathen tradition. We see it alive and well today in the Halloween custom of trick-or-treating. Halloween is the one modern holiday where there is still a universal understanding of its pagan origins. That visiting customs occurred year round in Europe, and that they are tied to the holiday with the strongest surviving pagan connotation lends credence to the pagan origins of door-to-door traditions.

So this is an example of where my methodology is to look for trends of continuity and congruence. If there is not hard evidence for a specific thing, is there evidence for a closely related thing that can be traced? And then, we use logic. Say there is no documented evidence for Christmas caroling before a certain date, but there is evidence that going door to door caroling was done at other holidays, that there is documented evidence that in other cases the custom is rooted in indigenous European practice, and we can prove that in other instances the practice has pagan origins. Logically, we can infer that the practice in question, because it has continuity and congruency with the other instances, is part of the same lexicon. In the case of Christmas caroling in particular, this inference can be bolstered by the corroborating evidence wherein the Church leaders tried to ban the custom during the early post-conversion eras. Obviously, if the practice had an origin within the Church, then the Church would not be trying to ban it. Logically, we can infer that if the Church is trying to stamp out a custom, then it must have origins outside of the church.

We can see that failure to use logical reasoning and instead hyper-focusing on documentation of a practice is an almost autistic-like absence of nuance in analysis. But, it does seem clear that historians in previous generations had an inherent bias which caused them to downplay the presence of European Native Faith due to their own Christian beliefs. On the same token, while neo-paganism is on the rise, the trend in academia is atheistic rationalism. There seems to be a tendency for atheistic rationalists to also attempt to downplay the presence of paganism.

The filter of bias is unavoidable. And critics will say that I myself, as a practitioner of European Native Faith, will be looking at this through my own filtered bias. This is really a universal truth which appears even among scientists. We cannot avoid our own biases. However, my beliefs evolved to adapt to what I was uncovering in my research into European folk belief, not the other way around. I was raised as a Christian and was sincere in that faith (as any child is, a child only knows what they are taught). In my early adulthood, I adopted an agnostic approach. Agnosticism seems to place less of a block on the serious thinker than does atheism. For an atheist is just like a monotheist in that they will auto-reject anything that violates their rigid view of the cosmos.

Agnosticism lends well to animistic polytheism because an agnostic's stance is "well, I don't know for sure, I'll look into it and think about it." When Europeans were free to be culturally whole, that is when their language, mythos, ethnicity, and culture were all one and the same, the worldview that is nurtured under such a holistic lifestyle is one that understands there are many layers of meaning, many realms of existence, many formats of consciousness, many different spirits who interact with us on all of these levels. So while someone with a more rigid ideological worldview might disagree, I think it was my agnostic openness that allowed me to see more in the available material as opposed to a vision which restricts and limits the viewfinder. On the same token, having dabbled with interest in many related disciplines also lends to a prism effect, whereas hyper-focusing through only one lends to tunnel vision.

Continuity and Congruence

This brings us to another point. Returning again to the topic of bias in historical vision, and the superimposition of Christian narratives over European indigenous holidays, it bears noting that virtually every single holiday in the European calendar year has Native Faith origins and is still rife with pagan imagery today. When I state that only Halloween is undisputed, what I mean by that is undisputed by lay people who do not have a strong grounding in history and whose view is colored by religious bias. That Christmas retained a plethora of Heathen imagery from the Teutonic holiday of Yule is well-known. Yet, one still finds historians arguing over the legitimacy of the Christmas tree as an ancient pagan custom due to the lack of hard evidence documenting its use in the pre-Christian era. But, as explained above, there very likely would not be "evidence" in the sense of written documentation for something like this.

When one looks at other holiday customs, we see a continuity in practice that lends to the veracity of the Christmas tree being an ancient custom. For instance, the

Yule log has a documented history in England, and it even retains the old pagan holiday's title in its name. The custom was popular in England (which carried Anglo-Saxon heritage, a Germanic people), whereby the family would bring a large log inside to burn for Yuletide. There were typically other ritual customs involved, such as decorating the log with beautiful garnishes and fragrant plants so that it would have an incense effect as it burned. In very large halls and homes, a whole tree trunk would function the Yule log. As time progressed, only the very wealthy had a large enough hearth to accommodate a tree trunk, but in early Anglo-Saxon tribal times, the custom was to live in communal family groups in longhouses with a large central hearth, a custom they shared with the Norse who continued the practice even longer. The Yule log was not simply fuel, it held sacred symbolic meaning as a special part of the Winter Solstice celebration. Indeed, we still see Yule log imagery in Christmas décor today. And, although the term "Yuletide" is not as common in the popular vernacular, one still hears it in popular Christmas songs, it appears in mainstream Christmas cards, and it was still quite popular in holiday media as recently as a century ago; thus attesting to the willingness of the European Native Faith to survive within a Christianized society.

In Germany today, a very similar custom to a decorated Christmas tree is enacted at Eastertide, wherein Germans hang colored eggs from trees outdoors. We also know from ancient Roman accounts that the pagan Germans worshipped their gods outdoors in sacred groves and that certain special trees were dedicated to gods; such as the famous Donar's Oak dedicated to Thor (Donar being the German equivalent to Scandinavian Thor). In addition, the ancient custom of wassailing the orchard trees can still be found in England today; wherein people gather in a fruit orchard (usually apple orchard) and enact a ritual designed to drive bad spirits away from the trees. They then give offerings to the trees so that they may bear fruit in abundance.

Therefore, we can see that trees live large in the Native Faith of the Teutons (and the wider Northern Europeans). Logically, it makes more sense that the

Christmas tree originated in this context and lived on than it does that Christians would invent a practice that has nothing at all to do with their religious meaning of the holiday. If we apply continuity and congruence, the Christmas tree fits in the Native European lexicon. It sticks out like a sore thumb in the Christian one.

      It is my strong opinion that when a folk custom fits congruently with other customs that have a more strongly documented point of origin, that lends to its veracity. If a custom stands out like a sore thumb or contradicts what we know about folk belief and practice, then that is a sign that it does not fit within the native European paradigm. Essentially, what we're trying to do here is reconstruct a picture that has been fragmented into puzzle pieces. To demand documentary or otherwise "hard" evidence when we've established all the reasons for the absence of evidence, is asinine. But when we have a piece that fits perfectly within the puzzle of one picture, but does not jibe at all with the other, at this point it's just common sense. And this methodology is important to understand for the following chapter

The Easter Controversy

While Halloween was the only holiday to remain overtly pagan and revel in that association, and Christmas retained the flavor, imagery, and customs of Yule but was given a Christian overlay, Easter is the major holiday that has had its origins the most disputed. Despite the overt presence of imagery associated with fertility (hares, rabbits, eggs, etc), the same argument discussed above is used to say that since there is no hard documentation of this imagery in pre-Christian times they must therefore be a more recent invention. Further, there have been many historians who have argued vehemently against the veracity of the goddess Eostre as a figure of veneration to the pagan Anglo-Saxons (Ostara to the Germans).

This particular subject could bear an entire book of intense study, so it is impossible to do it justice as a short chapter here. But, sufficed to say, there is a great deal of evidence to corroborate Eostre/Ostara as a Teutonic goddess associated with both the spring and the dawn. The

most obvious evidence is linguistic. In both English and German, the spring holiday still bears etymological cognate to her name; Easter is literally named after Eostre for English speakers, and in Germany the holiday is called Ostern after Ostara.

As explained, if a figure or custom is incongruent or anomalous to the lexicon of European belief, in other words if it doesn't fit, then it should be examined with scrutiny. But, Eostre/Ostara fits perfectly for many reasons. Not only is her name etymologically related to the name of the holiday itself, but it is cognate to other known and verified Aryan (Indo-European) goddesses with the same association. Easter, we can see, has the word "east" in the name, which is a nod to the direction from whence the sun rises. The word Ostern has the same tie to the word "east" in German.

If I have learned anything in my studies of the European folk tradition, it is that our ancient mythos functioned as a fluid fabric of many layers. Just as the year turns in a regular cycle, the day and night move in a regular cycle, as does life and death. The association of this deity with both east (dawn) and springtime is symbolic of life cycles. Springtime is the "dawn" of the year, where everything is bright and fresh, and new life begins again. This goddess heralds from the east with the dawning of each day, and brings the new life of the springtime. This same connotation can be seen in the Greek goddess Eos, Roman Aurora, and the Baltic Ausrine – all of which are linguistic cognates to one another and to Ostara/Eostre.

There is actually very early written documentation for Eostre. The English religious historian Bede made reference to her in the 8th century in his historical work called "The Ecclesiastical History of the English People." That should settle the debate, right? But, biased academics have long been arguing that Bede "invented" this goddess. Which is nonsensical. Why would a Christian scribe invent a pagan goddess when it was his goal to eradicate paganism? Even more absurd is the idea that a Christian historian would make sure that his invented goddess bore a name that is cognate to other European goddesses who also shared the same symbolic associations, as well as being cognate with the word "east" in order to embody the dawn connotation. In addition, if Bede invented this goddess, where did the name of the holiday come from? Why would the Church invent a fake pagan goddess and then name a Christian holiday after her, with a name that has nothing at all to do with the Christian meaning they were promoting? That simply does not make sense. It is literally illogical. A logical fallacy.

As if that shouldn't settle the debate on its own, it turns out that a Christian scribe in 9th century Germany corroborates Bede's account. Einhard was an educated historian who was in the service of the Frankish king Charlemagne. For those who don't know, the Franks were a Germanic tribe but by the time of Charlemagne they had long been Latinized. The Franks, therefore, stand at the crux of the Mediterranean acculturation of Northern Europe. Charlemagne, while he was a great defender of Europe against Islamicization, was also guilty of slaughtering thousands of Europeans and enforcing the new Mediterranean religion by the force of the sword. In "The Life of Charlemagne," Einhard mentions that the month of

April is known to the German Saxons as Oster-monath (Ôstarmânot).

This corroborates Bede's mentioning of April as Ēastermōnaþ (Easter month) to the Anglo-Saxons of England in the previous century. Again, we have to ask if it makes any sense at all that the English Bede would invent a goddess and claim that the month of April was named for her and that his trickery was so refined that he could predict that another scribe would record that Germanic cousins on the continent would have a linguistic cognate for the same month.

It gets to the point where the argument against Eostre's viability is very far-fetched. But, none the less, scholars have been arguing it vehemently for ages. It appears to be an example where evidence can be clear as day, but vision is so clouded by a filtered lens that the individual cannot see what is clearly evident. In my opinion, the Christian meaning ascribed to the Easter holiday is the crux of the entire Christian religion. Halloween could remain pagan because it was never given a new meaning that meant much to the Christian religious narrative. Christmas is, of course, important, as it was assigned as the day that Christ entered the world in human form. But, old Yuletide imagery did not threaten that story.

Easter, however, was re-packed as the date of Christ's resurrection; without which the entire religion becomes unhinged. Therefore, acknowledging that this

holiday was celebrated prior to Christianization and, even more poignantly, that a completely different figure was venerated is much more threatening to the Christian narrative than the presence of Santa Claus is at Christmas time. On a psychological level, it seems clear that this threat is so great that individuals who base their identity in Christianity literally cannot handle it. Therefore, there has been this impetus to deny her existence all together. If Eostre never existed, she cannot be a threat to the meaning of Easter.

There is, actually, much more evidence to support the existence of the figure of Eostre in the Teutonic consciousness. But, the information laid out here should clearly demonstrate to anyone how absurd the denial of the existence of this sacred figure is. And I am not asserting that she existed as a historical figure (such as arguments for a historical Jesus or Buddha), but rather her existence as a figure of veneration in the consciousness of the culture. The fact that we have documentary attestations, symbolic elements in modern folk practice that jibes with mytho-linguistic parallels, and linguistic evidence (and one linguistic scholar by the name of Philip Shaw has discussed even more evidence for Eostre's existence in his book, "Pagan Goddesses in the Early Germanic World"), should be enough to prove to any skeptic that this is a legitimate mythological figure with a place of importance to the English and German people.

There is, as stated, enough information on this topic that it deserves an entire book of exploration. But for the sake of space, we must move on. The point to take from this is to note how bias in academia has skewed views of history right along from both the point of the recording of propagandized history to the social and institutionalized biases inherent in academia which has influenced our views of history.

What is the European Folk-Soul?

What has been laid out in the preceding chapters has been a discussion on elements of European Native Faith that lived on side by side with Christianity right along through the ages. We also discussed reasons why this fact has been obscured by historians who refuse to see it for various reasons, and why it can be difficult to see. Nevertheless, our ancient mythos as represented by archetypes, imagery, traditions, even the language we use is still present with us to this very day.

In a way, the fact that these things lived on subconsciously is incredibly profound. It speaks to not only their power, but to how strongly embedded our Native Faith is in the European consciousness. It matters very little that the vast majority of European Britons, Germans, and Americans who descended from those cultures all identified as Christians for they still told their children that Santa Claus was coming to visit them as they slept at night in exactly the same way that ancient Europeans under their

indigenous worldview believed that their own gods and figures would visit the home for Yuletide. Not only that, but these Christian Europeans still taught their children to leave cookies and milk out for Santa Claus in the same way that Europeans practicing their indigenous folkways left out offerings of grains and dairy as an offering for domestic spirits and visiting spirits. This is the European Folk-Soul.

Likewise, these Europeans who called themselves Christians continue to this day to tell their children that the Easter Bunny had visited in the night leaving gifts filled with springtime fertility symbols. Their children squeal over chocolate eggs before going off to Easter Sunday church service. This is the European Folk-Soul.

How profound it is that our Folk-Soul lived on so vibrantly for centuries even through eras of brutal oppression. The new religion had to be enforced by sword and fire, and then continuously reinforced at the pulpit. There was no institution endorsing European native folkways. Quite the opposite, there were institutions actively suppressing it. Yet, here it is today still with us. This speaks to the veracity of our Folk-Soul. It is real whether we acknowledge it or not. It is part of us. It informs us as a culture. And even when there were violent repercussions for maintaining our folkways, we never let go. We found ways to carry on our traditions while simultaneously practicing the prescribed religion that we literally had no choice but to practice.

It does not matter if an individual is willing to acknowledge their own European Folk-Soul or not. We can see that psychological conditioning has been used to block the vision of many. If they can look at our holiday traditions and continue to deny the presence of European Native Faith in our culture, then they are blind. But their blindness does not negate the truth of this reality. The heart of our Folk-Soul continues to beat steadily whether we acknowledge it or not.

Our Folk-Soul
is our Salvation

That Christianity became part of the fabric of European culture is not in dispute. Although the motivation for its spread through Northern Europe can only honestly be said to disingenuous on a spiritual level due to its nature as a political campaign, it eventually was embraced with sincerity by the European people, even if due to lack of choice. The survival of Native European Faith as embodied by folk beliefs and traditional customs speaks to the veracity of the European cultural spirit. Our native identity and indigenous collective soul survived a foreign acculturation that was hoisted upon us from the top down. In fact, we forced the foreign religion to adapt to us and refused to let go of our native sacred imagery and customs. Our indigenous Folk-Soul remained vibrant and strong – even when we were not consciously aware of the origins and meanings of certain traditions.

Today, we see a new political agenda actively working to suppress ethnic-European culture. But, this threat is even more diabolical. Whereas Christianity moved north from the Mediterranean and pushed to unite Europeans into a globalist empire (the Catholic Church)

through a universalist ideology, the local people still kept their ethnic identities. Today, a very similar plan is being enacted by those with the power to manipulate the masses, but the tactic is different. The new tactic is to erase all sense of ethnic identity all together.

Although Christianity (whether Catholic or Protestant, and in many ways the Protestants were much, much worse than the R.C.C.) actively worked to suppress indigenous European folkways, it is clear that the European Folk-Soul survived. It may have survived a bit tattered and battle weary, but it survived. So due to this point, we can recognize that our ethnic-European brothers and sisters who find spiritual fulfillment in Christianity are still united with those of us who look toward our indigenous European roots; because whether they are aware on a conscious level or not, our indigenous folk soul is highly present in their own religious celebrations. Therefore we can still be united under the banner of ethnic-identity. If we can look past differences of religious ideology and remember that Christians and adherents of European Native Faith share the same European Folk-Soul, we can stand united to defend it together.

It seems clear that harping on religious identity has been a tool used to work against us for centuries. Making religion the primary definition of one's identity is a tactic to displace our ethnic identity. As mentioned at the beginning of this piece, throughout all of human history until the more recent "revealed" religions (especially the Abrahamic), language, race, culture, and mythos were ALL one and the same. We've been culturally fractured. And we've been distracted away from our ethnic bonds. Christianity functioned very much the same way we can see Islam working today to absorb adherents into a Borg-like state of assimilation wherein the adherents make their religion their primary self-identity, forsaking any other cultural precedence. Essentially, it's a donkey-carrot tactic. Religion has been waved like a carrot leading the donkey away from his herd. The herd, or rather, our tribe, must come first before all other distractions. For leading the donkey from the herd, or leading us away from our tribal identities, renders him vulnerable to the predator.

The time has come for every one of us to take a stand for our tribal identity as ethnic-Europeans first and foremost. For it is through our ethnic identity that we can find true unity irrespective of religion. If we have unity, and if we make our ethnic identity our main focus, we are unstoppable. And this is precisely why there is such a strong effort to erode, shame, and erase our ethnic pride today. The modern attacks on Christmas by Muslims and atheists today are as upsetting as the attacks on Yuletide by Christian authorities were in the past. But while Yule was suppressed, it never died. Its very spirit, imagery, traditions, and lore lived on in European Christmas.

Therefore an attack on Christmas is an attack on ALL Europeans, whether Christian or Heathen. And I will stand shoulder to shoulder with ethnic-European Christians to fight the attacks on Christmas because the Yuletide season is the modern heart of the European folk-soul. Whether you see the winter solstice season as the birth of the Son or the birth of the Sun is irrelevant to me. Whether you celebrate Jesus' journey to mankind or see Santa's journey as Wotan's Ride is irrelevant. Christmas is the prime example that demonstrates the comingling of pagan and Christian belief in European folkways. Both became our European identity as a hybrid. The attack on Christmas more than religious assault, it is literally a sword-thrust piercing the heart of the collective European soul.

Bibliography and Further Reading:

Baker, Margaret. Discovering Christmas Customs and Folklore. Buckhamshire: Shire Publications, 1999.

Bates, Brian. The Real Middle Earth. Oxford: Sidgwick& Jackson, 2002.

Coffin, Tristram P. The Book of Christmas Folklore. New York: The Seabury Press, 1973.

Davidson, Hilda Ellis. Roles of the Northern Goddess. London: Routledge, 1998. print.

Emerick, Carolyn. "The Hidden History of Christmas Carols." Celtic Guide (2013): 15-19.

Fletcher, Richard. The Barbarian Conversion: From Paganism to Christianity. Berkeley: University of California Press, 1997.

Owen, Trefor M. "The Celebration of Candlemas in Wales." Folklore 84.3 (1973): 238–251.

Salla, Sandra M. "Carols." Medieval Folklore. Ed. J. McNamara, and J. Lindow C. Lindahl. Oxford: Oxford University Press, 2002.

Shaw, Philip A. Pagan goddesses in the early Germanic world: Eostre, Hreda and the cult of matrons. London: Bristol Classical Press, 2011.

Simpson, Jacqueline. European Mythology. London: The Hamlyn Publishing Group, 1987.

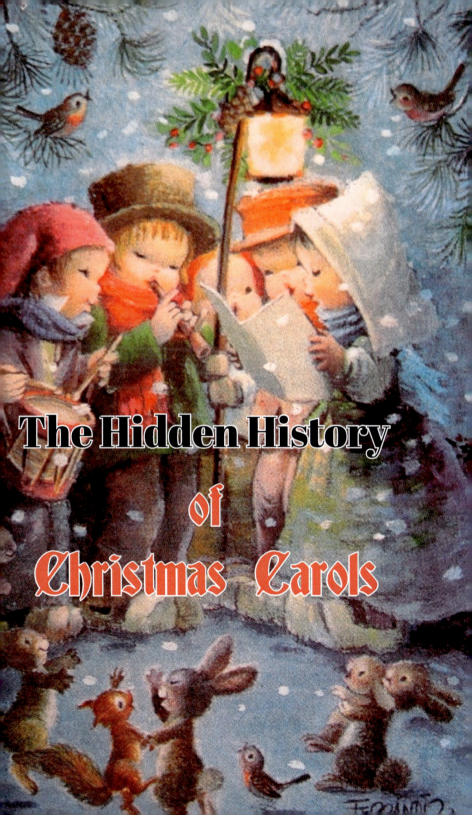

Chapter Contents

Introduction	33
Caroling's Naughty Past	35
Church Bans on "Pagan" Caroling	37
Door to Door Holiday Customs	39
The Christmas Tie to Halloween	40
The Christian Transformation	43
Caroling in the Modern Era	45
Bibliography & Further Reading	47

Introduction

A note to the reader: Never has it been so evident that history can sometimes be murky and difficult to wade through than during my quest to discover the roots of Christmas caroling! Different sources give different information, conflicting dates, and varying histories.

Ordinarily I would not open with a disclaimer. But, under the circumstances, if the reader were to look up this information on their own, they might find answers different than what I've written here. So, I will endeavor to weed through it all and give my own assessment of the material. And, I will try to be clear about where my information came from by citing all sources. - Carolyn

The story of Christmas caroling is full of unexpected surprises. The practice itself has gone through many changes over the centuries, and our perception of caroling today is based only on very recent history. We think of Christmas caroling as a wholesome, and even religious, activity. Caroling seems to speak of the beauty, innocence, and magic of the Christmas season. However, in researching this practice, I have discovered that caroling was not as innocent as we might think. In fact, the act of caroling was actively combated by the Church for hundreds of years.

Uncovering the origins of caroling has proven difficult. Some sources give the 14th or 15th centuries as the earliest known date of the practice. I believe the reason for this is because this is the period when caroling began to be adopted by the church, and therefore this is when carols first began to be written down. However, there is much evidence that caroling was around long before that. We don't have written carols from the early periods, but what we do have are edicts from the Church and recorded sermons which make reference to caroling.

Carolers dancing in a medieval manuscript

Caroling's Naughty Past

In his book, The Book of Christmas Folklore, Tristram P. Coffin says that "For seven centuries a formidable series of denunciations and prohibitions was fired forth by Catholic authorities, warning Everyman to 'flee wicked and lecherous songs, dancings, and leapings'" (p98).

Apparently early carols could be quite lewd, and they were originally associated with dance as well as song. The caroling dancers often went around town in costume, and it is related to the custom of mumming.

Coffin mentions that this revelry was considered so offensive to the Church that they referred to caroling as "sinful traffic" and issued decrees against it in 1209 A.D. and 1435 A.D. It must have been a good time, for clerics and priests who found themselves caught up in the fun received a stern scolding.

Medieval revelry, illustration from a medieval manuscript

The Church viewed these activities as "very remnant of pagan custom" (p99). But, more than that, the street revelry could get out of control. Alcohol was usually flowing during caroling festivities, and drunken singers could get rowdy and even violent.

"When a fellow named Gilbert de Foxlee tried to break up the dancing, he was stabbed in the back with a dagger, cut in the right arm with a sword, and slashed on the left leg with an axe. He died after eight weeks of infection and pain" (Coffin, p 99). Evidently carolers were well armed!

A naughty drunken medieval monk

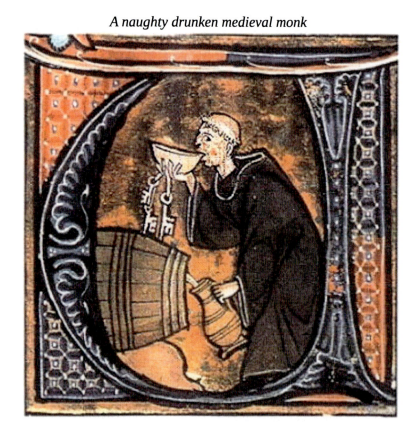

Church Bans on "Pagan" Caroling

Sandra M. Salla is a contributor to a fantastic resource called Medieval Folklore, an encyclopedia of folkloric terms. In her entry for "Carols," Salla says that "between 600 and 1500 C.E. the Church formally banned the dancing of carols on church grounds" and that numerous informal "decrees, sermons, and exempla were written condemning the activity" (Salla, p61).

While some authors attribute caroling to purely Christian origins, and begin the history of caroling with those written down in a Christian context, this is contradicted by the evidence. We can see that the Church long considered it a pagan practice, as evidenced by the wording in the edicts condemning caroling.

Medieval mummers on a British stamp

Also, that Salla mentions the edicts against caroling begin in the 6th century is telling. The 6th and 7th centuries were the period of conversion for the Anglo-Saxons in England. The fact that edicts against caroling begin to appear in the record at the same time as the conversion period is circumstantial evidence hinting that caroling had pagan roots and was in existence long before conversion. But, those records do not explain why caroling was considered to have pagan connotations.

Jacqueline Simpson, a scholar who specializes in mediaeval English and Scandinavian history, explores this in her wonderful book, European Mythology. Simpson explains that it can sometimes be difficult to determine which customs actually stem from pagan tradition because Church clerics were quick to condemn almost anything as pagan

She explains that customs involving drunkenness, cross dressing (usually in play acting and carnival type festivities), or elements that expressed sexuality were described as "devilish" even if there was no devil involved (Simpson, p118).

Vintage Christmas card

Door to Door
Holiday Customs

One example of a song and dance tradition similar to caroling that has an overt connection to paganism is in Romanian Căluş dance which has survived into modern times. Participants dress in costume, like modern mummers and early carolers, and go around the village singing and dancing.

The Căluşari, members of the all-male dance troupe, were once a secret society which appears to have been openly associated with paganism, and their members were exempt from partaking in mass. This group of dancers had another purpose other than entertainment.

They were said to possess secret charms of healing, and were known for banishing evil spirits. The Căluşari went door to door during mid-Winter offering their services and expected to be welcomed and generously compensated. If a home refused them entry, a curse would befall the homeowner (Simpson, pp121-126).

Weston Mummers who performed at the Packhorse Inn, Southstoke (England), on Boxing Day 2007. Photo in the public domain.

The Christmas Tie to Halloween

If this reminds you of Halloween, there's a good reason for that! The mid-Winter holiday we now call Christmas, but which was known as Yule in pre-Christian England and various other names in different cultures, was known to be a period of high spiritual activity – just as old Samhain was. This notion has faded away in our modern perception of Christmas, but it lingered on in Halloween.

European folklore is full of references to spiritual activity during Yule-tide. In fact, it was regarded as a spiritually dangerous time in both Celtic and Germanic cultures. So, it is not that far of a stretch to wonder if the Romanian Călușari tradition (which lasted well into the 19th century and perhaps later) gives us a glimpse of the earlier mumming and caroling traditions and we may speculate on the long lost spiritual connotations.

Further, just as the Călușari expect a reward or threaten a curse (literally trick or treat) early caroling traditions are almost always associated with demanding to be rewarded with food and drink or risk some kind of retribution.

Contemporary carolers still sing "Here we go a-wassailing" wherein there is a line requesting "now bring us some figgy pudding" and carolers threaten "we won't go until we get some." A survey of medieval carols will demonstrate that the request for food and drink is not unique to this song. Wassailing, a medieval synonym for caroling, is itself a reference to the alcoholic beverage wassail.

The word derives from the Old English term "waes-heal" meaning "good health," a greeting or toast (Baker, p83). Wassail is a medieval mulled wine (heated with spices) which was commonly served to carolers.

Vintage illustration featuring Father Christmas with a bowl of steaming wassail

Another reason to consider that there may be some connection between caroling and trick-or-treating is that caroling was done throughout the year, not simply at Christmas. This is mentioned in numerous sources, and there are accounts of caroling at other holidays in early folklore journals.

One article of particular interest is The Celebration of Candlemas in Wales, by Trefor M. Owen. In this scholarly article about the Candlemas holiday the word "carol" is mentioned seventy-two times, emphasizing the overwhelming evidence of caroling during a holiday other than Christmas. Candlemas is another holiday with known pagan origins, being the Christianized version of the old Celtic pagan Imbolc.

Owen shares one account of Welsh Candlemas caroling wherein the revelers go around town and sing outside of homes. This sounds innocent enough… at first. What ensues is the carolers sing bawdy songs about the Virgin Mary (no wonder the Church considering caroling sacrilegious!) and hurl insults at the home-owners! The home-owners are then obliged to return the insults to the carolers. Whichever group out-wits the other in verse would be declared the winner. If the revelers won, they must be allowed inside and given food and beverage (Owen pp242-243). And, interestingly, Owen mentions that wassailing was done at Halloween as well as Christmas and Candlemas and other holidays (p247).

So, we have a caroling tradition that involves costumes and demanding reward in the form of food or a risk threat. And, we also discover that caroling was done on Halloween in Britain. Could modern trick-or-treating and Christmas caroling have evolved from the same root practice many hundreds of years ago?

The Christian Transformation

The practice of caroling went through a transformation between the High Middle Ages (12th and 13th centuries) and the Renaissance period. As explained, the Church categorically rejected the practice due to the "close relationship between 'heathen dancing' and witchcraft" (Coffin, p99).

Eventually, church leaders adopted an "if you can't beat 'em, join 'em" approach. St. Francis of Assisi was one of the major proponents of replacing the old "riotous carols with ones more appropriate" in Italy, which then spread through Europe (Coffin, pp99-100). This led to a "great age of carol writing" between the years 1400 to 1650 (Baker, p81). But, during the same period caroling was actively suppressed by the Puritans (insert joke about Puritans always ruining all the fun here).

A little known fact about the history of witch trials is that caroling came up in trial testimony. Salla says "in witchcraft trials of the sixteenth century and later, accused witches often confessed to caroling" (p62).

Interestingly, just as witches were accused of inverting Christian practices like the mass and Sabbath rituals, there was apparently some notion of a witch's carol, which inverted the carol song and dance commonly practiced by the rest of the peasantry (Salla, p62).

A vintage Christmas card featuring a witch. Witches feature prominently in European holiday imagery to this day. The Christmas witch La Befana is the gift bringer to italian children. Witches are associated with Easter in Sweden, and with May Day in Germany.

Caroling in the Modern Era

Caroling evolved much over the years and seems to have gone through many stages. With the end of one stage came the beginning of another. The Puritans and their influence faded, and the Victorian Era began. The Victorians had a penchant for romanticizing and idealizing nostalgic customs of the past. And so, while other aspects of caroling such as its association with dance and other holidays faded away, the Victorians kept it very much alive at Christmas, albeit in a version very tame compared to the original.

It is only in recent years that the popularity of Christmas caroling has become in danger of extinction all together. Today the custom is mostly seen in shopping malls sung by children or church groups. Will caroling disappear from Western culture all together? Maybe it's time reintroduce the wassail and liven up the party!

Bibliography

Baker, Margaret (1999). Discovering Christmas Customs and Folklore. Buckinghamshire: Shire Publications.

Coffin, Tristram P. (1973). The Book of Christmas Folklore. New York: The Seabury Press.

Owen, Trefor M. (1973). The Celebration of Candlemas in Wales. Folklore, Vol. 84(3), pp. 238- 251.

Salla, Sandra M. (2002). Carols. In C. Lindahl, J. McNamara, and J. Lindow (Editors), Medieval Folklore (pp61-62). Oxford: Oxford University Press.

Simpson, Jacqueline (1987). European Mythology. Middlesex: The Hamlyn Publishing Group.

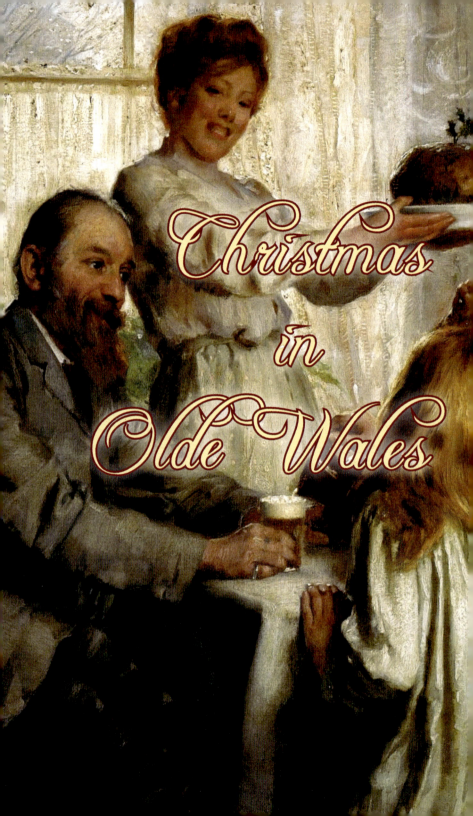

Chapter Contents

Y Gwyliau: The Midwinter Holiday	50
Trick or Treat at Christmas?	53
Wassailing with a Hobby Horse	56
Plygain – Watching the Dawn	58
Music and Song	59
Bibliography and Further Reading	62

Y Gwyliau: the Mid-Winter Holiday

Accounts of Christmas in Wales confirm that, like in other parts of Britain and the wider Europe, Christmas was a full season not just one special day. There were a variety of holy days and customs found throughout the Yuletide season. In a chapter called "Seasonal Festivities" from her book "Welsh Traditional Music," Phyllis Kinney says:

> *"Early in the eighteenth century, Wales was almost entirely rural. It was a country on the fringe of Europe without cities or a capital and with a small population – more people lived in London than in the whole of Wales – which was largely dependent on agriculture and ruled by the seasons."*

This means certain seasonal traditions could linger on in Wales while other parts of Britain had moved on, making Wales a window into the past.

Due to the heavily rural nature of Welsh life, most of the festivities still took place in the homes that dotted the countryside. Even the traditional agricultural lifestyle, though it consisted of hard work, still contrived to bring the folk together, and then traditional folk customs, tales, and songs could be shared even while hard at work sheering sheep, reaping harvest, or preparing food stuffs. This lifestyle meant that tradition was interwoven with the very fabric of Welsh life and worldview.

That time of year that we refer to as "the Christmas Season" today was called *Y Gwyliau* in Welsh, meaning simply "The Holidays." This encompassed about three weeks of rest and revelry where very little farm work was done.

It was common for farmhouses to have a "table room," *rwˆm ford* in Welsh, where farm hands would be welcomed to drink beer and feast as they roamed from farm to farm. Farmhands placed their ploughs under the tables as they feasted, and interestingly, they appear to have given an offering of beer to their ploughs before they had a sip themselves. This is supposed to be in thanks of the ploughs' service through the year and recognition that though they are still for now, they will be needed again soon.

This act seems to be a remnant from pre-Christian indigenous European worldview which saw the world in a more animistic light. Everything is imbued with a spirit and those spirits must be propitiated if their positive intercession is to be expected.

Vintage image of Christmas in Wales

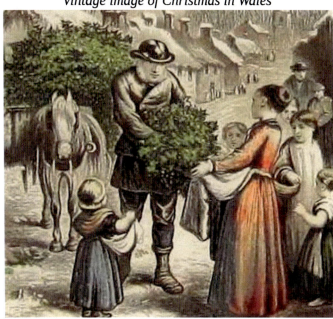

Farm hands eating with harvesters, by Jacopo Bassano

 at Christmas?

A tradition that struck me as exceptionally noteworthy is called "Thomassing." This might be passed over with a cursory glance by others, but after reading a great deal on folk customs over the years I have noticed a pattern that no one else seems to be discussing, so first some background information.

This is the custom of going door to door asking for food stuffs at sacred times of the year. It is remembered today in the American custom of Halloween "trick or treating," which was brought over with Scots-Irish immigrants.

What most people do not realize is that this custom was not relegated only to Halloween. Previously, I wrote piece called "The Hidden History of Christmas Carols" which discusses the similarity between Christmas caroling and trick or treating.

Traditionally, Christmas carolers used to ask for food in return for their carols. Just as trick-or-treaters threaten a "trick" if you don't give them a treat, Christmas carolers historically were quite a quite rowdy, even drunken, lot. This custom was likely very widespread throughout Europe, a Romanian version is discussed in my piece on Christmas carols.

Interestingly, this door to door visiting custom is found very strongly in Wales. While Halloween trick-or-treat is attributed to Scots-Irish tradition, the door to door custom has been recorded in Wales at both Christmas and

Candlemas.

In addition to the door to door custom occurring at holidays other than Halloween, it is also noted that caroling occurred at holidays other than Christmas. While this likely happened throughout Britain, and indeed Europe, it was recorded specifically in Wales. Excerpt from my "Christmas Carols":

One article of particular interest is 'The Celebration of Candlemas in Wales," by Trefor M. Owen. In this scholarly article about the Candlemas holiday the word "carol" is mentioned seventy-two times, emphasizing the overwhelming evidence of caroling during a holiday other than Christmas. Candlemas is another holiday with known pagan origins, being the Christianized version of the old Celtic pagan Imbolc.

Owen shares one account of Welsh Candlemas caroling wherein the revelers go around town and sing outside of homes. This sounds innocent enough… at first. What ensues is the carolers sing bawdy songs about the Virgin Mary (no wonder the Church considering caroling sacrilegious!) and hurl insults at the home-owners! The homeowners are then obliged to return the insults to the carolers. Whichever group out-wits the other in verse would be declared the winner. If the revelers won, they must be allowed inside and given food and beverage (Owen pp242-243).

And, interestingly, Owen mentions that wassailing was done at Halloween as well as Christmas and Candlemas and other holidays (p247). (Carolyn Emerick, "The Hidden History of Christmas Carols").

Jacqueline Simpson discusses "Thomassing" in her book "The Folklore of the Welsh Border." The practice was called "Thomassing" because it occurred on St. Thomas'

Day, the 21st of December. The poor women of the area would go door to door carrying a large sack, or some other receptacle, and ask for food staples such as grains, cheese, etc. The practice was also called "gooding" or "corning." Those names, I would guess, would have to do with seeking the good will of neighbors to share some corn, which in Britain means grain. In many regions, poor families would receive free grain and then the local miller would ground it free of charge so that each family could have cakes for Christmas day.

A Welshman celebrating St David's Day c. 1735, by Philip Mould

Wassailing
with a Hobby Horse

Mari Lwyd is universally considered to have native European (pre-Christian) roots and was adapted by the Church. The word means "Grey Mare" for its association with horses. It was once widespread through Wales but has mainly been seen in recent history in Llangynwyd near Maesteg (although it is being revived elsewhere in Wales).

On New Year's Day another door to door procession occurs, wherein a horse's skull is propped up on a pole, decorated with streaming ribbons, and draped with a white cloth. The skull is decorated with false eyes and ears.

Mari Lwyd, public domain, circa 1900

At each house the revelers recite rhyming verse at those who dwell inside. Those inside respond in verse and refuse to let the *Mari Lwyd* enter until a rhyming battle of words (and insults) ensues. This is remarkably similar to Wassailing and Trick or Treating as discussed above and in more detail in "The Hidden History of Christmas Carols."

Mari Lwyd in Wales, circa 1910

Plygain: Watching the Dawn

The custom of *Plygain* is mentioned in both Jacqueline Simpson's "European Mythology," and in Wirt Sikes' "British Goblins: Welsh Folk-lore, Fairy Mythology, Legends and Traditions." Sikes says that it was popular in Wales to gather at church at three in the morning. Everyone would hold small green candles designed specifically for this purpose. Whereas Simpson says that they gathered at five or six a.m.

Sometimes the meetings occurred at farms or in cottages. But, in any event, the people gathered to sing carols as the dawn arose in the sky. There are many old attempts to explain this custom. But, it seems tied into the recognition of the importance of the Winter Solstice as a turning point in the year, in my opinion.

Midnight Mass by Clarence Gagnon

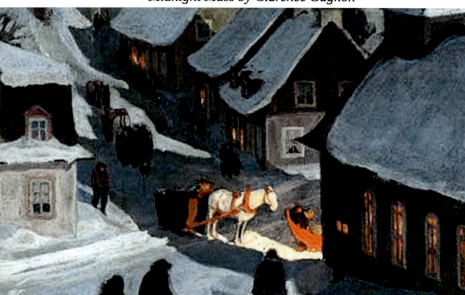

Music & Song

It would be remiss to discuss Welsh holiday festivities without a mention of Welsh musical tradition. It has been glossed over in each of these other traditions explored herein that song was a part of nearly all of the Welsh holiday festivities.

When the peasantry gathered for seasonal work, they often sang together. When they went door to door, whether carrying a decorated horse's head or to beg for grain, song was often a present element. And, when the folk gathered early on Christmas morning to watch the sun rise, they sang Christmas carols together.

The Wassail customs found in England had their own counterparts in Wales, to be sure. At Yuletide, when the Wassail bowl is passed round, people of all European nations imbibe of the jolly nectars of the season. So, I should like to leave you with a rhyme that I found while researching this article:

> *"When an Englishman is drunk he is belligerent;*
> *when a Frenchman is drunk he is amorous;*
> *when an Italian is drunk he is loquacious;*
> *when a Scotchman is drunk he is argumentative;*
> *when a German is drunk he is sleepy;*
> *when an American is drunk he brags;*
> *and when a Welshman is drunk he sings."*

Welsh Wassail Bowl, dated 1834. Note the many finger loops so that the jug could be passed around and everyone could share a swig.

Wales, like Scotland, will feature traditions that have influences in both the pagan Celtic and Anglo-Saxon cultures, as well as customs that developed in the more recent Christian era. Additionally, there are features that are distinctly Welsh. Most of Britain is a tapestry woven by these shared influences. In parts of the British Isles, Danish and Norse heritage is thrown into the mix, peppered by regional elements that give distinct local flavor.

So whether you carry Welsh ancestry in your family or not, I hope you can find some inspiration for keeping old European folk traditions alive in your household this holiday.

Image from "Christmas Sunshine" published in 1913 by the Hayes Lithographing Co.

Bibliography
& Further Reading

Emerick, Carolyn. "The Hidden History of Christmas Carols." Celtic Guide (2013): 15-19.

Johnson, Ben. Welsh Christmas Traditions. n.d. <http://www.historic-uk.com/HistoryUK/HistoryofWales>.

Kinney, Phillys. Welsh Traditional Music. Cardiff: Univ. of Wales Press, 2011.

Owen, Trefor M. "The Celebration of Candlemas in Wales." Folklore 84.3 (1973): 238–251.

Sikes, Wirt. British Goblins: Welsh Folk-lore, Fairy Mythology, Legends and Traditions. London: William Clowes and Sons, 1880.

Simpson, Jacqueline. The Folklore of the Welsh Border. London: B. T. Batsford Ltd, 1976.

Chapter Contents

Introduction	65
Ye Olde Christmas Carols	66
Auld Lang Syne & the Holiday Spirit	73
Ballade of Christmas	76
Customs from Cornwall	78
Christmas in Yorkshire	80

Introduction

This booklet is a collection of curated content. Presented herein are traditional songs that hearken back to days of old as well as accounts of holiday customs from Britain. The Christmas season is filled with imagery, music, tales, and customs that have roots in old European heritage. Many customs and carols originated long before they were ever recorded and many, if not most, have their roots in the indigenous beliefs of pre-Christian Europeans.

We live in a precarious age. Western society is teetering on the cusp of complete annihilation. This is one of those moments in time when we as a culture must pause for reflection. Will we let our heritage slip away? Or will we proudly assert that our heritage is worthy of preserving? For this reason, taking a moment to glimpse our own sacred heritage and remember that we, too, are indigenous peoples is so important.

With that in mind, I bring you a glimpse at how some of our ancestors celebrated the Yuletide Season and encourage everyone reading to consider how they can keep European tradition alive throughout the year, but especially at Christmastide.

Illustration from "Twas the Night Before Christmas" by Clement Moore illustrated by Jessie Willcox Smith 1912

Ye Olde Christmas Carols

The first piece I have for you is a Medieval Christmas Carole called "The Boar's Head." It is thought to be of German origin, but it was sung in England during the Middle Ages. This is especially interesting because it hearkens back to the days of old Yule before the changeover to Christmas. The boar was a sacred animal to Germanic pagans, and therefore also to the Anglo-Saxons who were of Germanic origin. Many people still eat ham on Christmas today, which is a remnant of the old pagan custom of sacrificing a boar for the Yule feast at Winter Solstice. The boar is also associated with the Teutonic god Freyr who was a hugely important figure to virtually all the Teutonic peoples from Scandinavia to mainland Germany to Anglo-Saxon England. Freyr was also called "Ing" and is remembered in many Germanic names that contain this element, such as Ingraham.

The Boar's Head

recorded approx. 1500, but estimated to be much older

The boris hed in hondes I brynge,
(The boar's head in hands I bring,)

with garlondes gay & byrdes syngynge!
(with garlands gay & birds singing!)

I pray you all, help me to synge, Qui estis in convivio!
(I pray you all, help me to sing, who are at this banquet!)

The boris hede I vnderstande
(The boar's head I understand,)

Ys cheffe seruyce in all this londe!
(Is chief service in all this land!)

Wher so ever it may be fonde, Seruitur cum sinapio!
(Whersoever it may be found, it is served with mustard!)

The boris hede I dare well say,
(The boar's head I dare well say,)

Anon after the XIIth Day,
(Anon after the twelfth day,)

He taketh his leve & goth a way! Exiuit tunc depatria!
(He takes his leave and goes away! He went out from his native country!)

The Wassail Song

The "Wassail Song" is a Christmas Carol that appears to have its origins in the Victorian Era, although its authorship is unknown. Whether this song has earlier incarnations that simply were never recorded (or were lost to time), the custom of wassailing itself dates to indigenous pre-Christian Britain. As explored in "The Hidden History of Christmas Carols," door to door visiting customs are found widespread across the European landscape. The word "wassail" came from the Anglo-Saxon term *was hál* which was a greeting that wished good health to the recipient. The word became associated with the mulled cider beverage of the same name, with the door to door visiting custom we now call "caroling," and with a pagan fertility rite that was performed in apple orchards to propitiate the spirits of the apple trees.

Here we come a-wassailing
Among the leaves so green;
Here we come a-wand'ring
So fair to be seen.

REFRAIN:
Love and joy come to you,
And to you your wassail too;
And God bless you and send you a Happy New Year
And God send you a Happy New Year.

Our wassail cup is made
Of the rosemary tree,
And so is your beer
Of the best barley.

REFRAIN

We are not daily beggars
That beg from door to door;
But we are neighbours' children,
Whom you have seen before.

REFRAIN

Call up the butler of this house,
Put on his golden ring.
Let him bring us up a glass of beer,
And better we shall sing.

REFRAIN

We have got a little purse
Of stretching leather skin;
We want a little of your money
To line it well within.

REFRAIN

Bring us out a table
And spread it with a cloth;
Bring us out a mouldy cheese,
And some of your Christmas loaf.

REFRAIN

God bless the master of this house
Likewise the mistress too,
And all the little children
That round the table go.

REFRAIN

Good master and good mistress,
While you're sitting by the fire,
Pray think of us poor children
Who are wandering in the mire.

REFRAIN

The Hogmanay Song

Now we journey to the Isle of Skye. This is an untitled Hogmanay song that was also published in the journal *Folklore*. Mary Julia MacCulloch included this in her article "Folk-Lore of the Isle of Skye" printed in 1923. This song is no doubt much older.

Hogmanay is the New Year's celebration in Scotland. The origins of the word are obscure and there are many different theories. Some scholars believe it to be a corruption of the Greek *hagia mena*, meaning holy month, while others ascribe a Gaelic or Norse origin. In my view, it may be one of those cultural traditions that is distinctly Scots while perhaps being a synthesis of the other European cultural influences mentioned. Another such word is the Manx "Hop-tu-naa" describing the Halloween holiday on the Isle of Man. Some scholars ascribe a Celtic language origin, while others insist that the origin is unclear. Both holidays have their own associated songs and traditions.

In recent years, the city of Edinburgh has been seen celebrating Hogmanay with Viking reenactments and a dramatic ship burning. This seems to be borrowed from the Shetland Islands' tradition of "Up-Helly-Aa," another end of the year celebration. Interestingly, there seems to be no disagreement about the origins of this term being rooted in Old Norse language. Although Shetland is part of Scotland today, its heritage largely Scandinavian. While Gaelic was retained mainly in the Scottish Highlands and the Hebridean Islands, many of the Hebrides isles were also conquered by Viking invaders. In fact, several Scottish clans from the Western Isles trace their origins to a Norse chieftain. So it is possible that the funny names of these other holidays, Hogmanay and Hop-tu-naa, also have a Norse influence.

A Christmas, A Christmas,
A Happy New Year,
A pocketful of money
And a barrelful of beer.

God bless the master of this house,
God bless the mistress too
And all the little children
That round the table go.

Hogmanay, Hogmanay,
Give us a penny and let us away,
If you haven't a penny, a ha'penny will do,
If you haven't a ha'penny, God bless you.

As I went down the river side
The river gave a jump,
If you've anything within the house
Give us a big lump.

*Viking longship burning for Hogmanay in Edinburgh.
Photo by Lee Kindness.*

Auld Lang Syne & the Holiday Spirit

What truly makes Christmas special are the traditions that we participate in year after year. Some customs are participated in by the wider culture, and others are unique to individual families. One unique aspect of the Christmas holiday is that traditions travel. European-American Christmas traditions have been adopted by all corners of the world. And many diverse elements from different European cultures traversed great distances to make their mark in far away places.

Yet, even when a family lights up their German Christmas tree, awaits the jingling of Finnish sleigh bells, and gathers to sing the Scots song *Auld Lang Syne*, they will incorporate elements of their own cultural background into their Christmas feast. An Italian-American family I knew well had been in America long enough to forget *La Befana*, the female witch who is the bringer of gifts in Italy, but not long enough to phase out three kinds of pasta dishes with home-made sauce and meatballs from their Christmas dinner. My own family enjoyed a raisin and cinnamon bread pudding inherited from my British great-grandparents, and the children always received Advent calendars holding a surprise for each day leading up to Christmas from our German heritage grandmother.

These traditions form the memories that are what bond us together within the family and within the wider culture. *Auld Lang Syne,* by Robert Burns captures this sentiment perfectly. It is a song that is sung by many, but understood by few. According to Merriman Webster's dictionary, the phrase literally translates as "old long ago," but the meaning is more accurately expressed by the modern phrase "the good old times" or "for old time's sake." The song is most synonymous with New Year's Eve, but is also sung at graduations, funerals, or any time we are looking backward with nostalgia. Due to the New Year's connotation, the song has become a symbol of the holiday season and the joy of togetherness that the holidays bring.

While our modern lives become ever more fragmented and separated from what we once held dear, coming home for Christmas to spend time with loved ones really does evoke the emotion expressed in Robert Burns' famous song. This holiday season, start a new tradition that can be looked back on in years to come. And, keep your own family traditions alive… for *auld lang syne*.

Burns' Original Scots	**Modern English Version**
Should auld acquaintance be forgot,	Should old acquaintance be forgot,
and never brought to mind?	and never brought to mind?
Should auld acquaintance be forgot,	Should old acquaintance be forgot,
and auld lang syne?	and old lang syne?
CHORUS:	CHORUS:
For auld lang syne, my jo, for auld lang syne,	For auld lang syne, my dear, for auld lang syne,
we'll tak a cup o' kindness yet,	we'll take a cup of kindness yet,
for auld lang syne.	for auld lang syne.
And surely ye'll be your pint-stowp!	And surely you'll buy your pint cup!
and surely I'll be mine!	and surely I'll buy mine!
And we'll tak a cup o' kindness yet,	And we'll take a cup o' kindness yet,

for auld lang syne.

CHORUS

We twa hae run about the braes,

and pu'd the gowans fine;

But we've wander'd mony a weary fit,

sin auld lang syne.

CHORUS

We twa hae paidl'd i' the burn,

frae morning sun till dine;

But seas between us braid hae roar'd

sin auld lang syne.

CHORUS

And there's a hand, my trusty fiere!

and gie's a hand o' thine!

And we'll tak a right gude-willy waught,

for auld lang syne.

CHORUS

for auld lang syne.

CHORUS

We two have run about the slopes,

and picked the daisies fine;

But we've wandered many a weary foot,

since auld lang syne.

CHORUS

We two have paddled in the stream,

from morning sun till dine;

But seas between us broad have roared

since auld lang syne.

CHORUS

And there's a hand my trusty friend!

And give me a hand o' thine!

And we'll take a right good-will draught,

for auld lang syne.

CHORUS

Ballade of Christmas

"Ballade of Christmas" was found in an old journal called Irish Monthly, from 1905. The author is known only by his initials, J.W.A.

Hang up the holly, nor forget
The waxen-berried mistletoe;
What matter if the wind be wet
And roads be slushed with melting snow ?
The lamplight's gleam, the yule-log's glow,
Shall brighten all the hours that glide,
And we will bless them as they go
The merry days of Christmastide.

The clouded sun makes haste to set,
The feet of night are overslow,
-The bare bough shivers, black as jet,
While gusty winter's breezes blow;
But on our hearts no gloom can throw
Its shadow, where glad thoughts abide:
We sing our stave and laugh, Ho! Ho!
The merry days of Christmastide!

Banished awhile are cares that fret,
Sad memories of grief and woe;
We make a truce with old regret
And bitter tears of long ago:
Such cares may come, such tears may flow
Before the winter shall have died;
But cares and tears must never know
The merry days of Christmastide.
Friend, Father Time may bend his bow

To slay our pleasures in their pride;
His malice cannot conquer so
The merry days of Christmastide.

Customs from Ye Olde Cornwall

Many customs from days gone by are no longer remembered by those in both the New World or the Old Countries. By digging through antique folklore accounts, we can glimpse the world of our ancestors, and maybe find inspiration for new family traditions inspired by the old. A Folk-Lore Journal entry from 1886, by M. A. Courtney, describes holiday customs from Cornwall:

In Cornwall, as in the other English counties, the houses are at Christmas "dressed up" with evergreens, sold in small bunches, called " Penn'orths of Christmas"; and two hoops fastened one in the other by nails at the centres are gaily decorated with evergreens, apples, oranges, &c., and suspended from the middle beam in the ceiling of the best kitchen.

This is the "bush," or " kissing bush." At night a lighted candle is put in it, stuck on the bottom nail; but once or twice lately I have seen a Chinese lantern hanging from the top one. This is an innovation.

In a few remote districts on Christmas-eve children may be, after nightfall, occasionally (but rarely) found dancing -around painted lighted candles placed in a box of sand. This custom was very general fifty years ago.

When open chimneys were universal in farmhouses the Christmas stock, mock, or block (the log), on which a rude figure of a man had been chalked, was kindled with great ceremony; in some parts with a piece of a charred wood that had been saved from the last year's "block."

A log in Cornwall is almost always called a "block." "Throw a block on the fire." Candles painted by some member of the family were often lighted at the same time.

At the plentiful supper always provided on this night, egg-hot, or eggy-hot, was the principal drink. It was made with eggs, hot beer, sugar, and rum, and was poured from one jug into another until it became quite white and covered with froth.

A sweet giblet pie was one of the standing dishes at a Christmas dinner-a kind of mince-pie, into which the giblets of a goose, boiled and finely chopped, were put instead of beef. Cornwall is noted for its pies, that are eaten on all occasions; some of them are curious mixtures, such as squab-pie, which is made with layers of well-seasoned fat mutton and apples, with onions and raisins.

Mackerel pie: the ingredients of this are mackerel and parsley stewed in milk, then covered with a paste and baked. When brought to table a hole is cut in the paste, and a basin of clotted cream thrown in it. Muggetty pie, made from sheep's entrails (muggets), parsley, and cream.

"The devil is afraid to come into Cornwall for fear of being baked in a pie."

Christmas in Yorkshire

The last piece I have for you brings us back to Olde Yorkshire. This is an excerpt from an article called "Folklore from Yorkshire" by J. B. Partridge. It was published in the journal Folklore *in 1914, and it discusses some of the old traditions that still survived at the time it was written.*

Christmas Observances in Yorkshire

Furmety is still eaten on Christmas Eve in Swaledale. The corn with which it is made is a present from the grocer.

Sword dancers still go round on Christmas Eve, dancing and singing a song about "Poor old horse."

The Yule log is generally given. It is brought into the house after dusk on Christmas Eve, and is at once put on the hearth. It is unlucky to have to light it again after it has once been started, and it ought not to go out until it has burned away. To sit round the Yule log and tell ghost stories is a great thing to do on this night, also card-playing.

Two large coloured candles are a Christmas present from the grocer. Just before supper on Christmas Eve (when furmety is eaten), while the Yule log is burning, all other lights are put out,and the candles are lighted from the Yule log by the youngest person present. While they are being lighted, all are silent and wish. The wish must not be told, but you see if you get it during the year. As soon as the candles are on the table, silence may be broken. They must be allowed to burn themselves out, and no other lights may be lighted that night.

Some people, especially cottagers, put a ring, thimble, and six-pence into the Christmas cake. (*From Mrs. Day, Minchinhampton, a native of Swaledale.*)

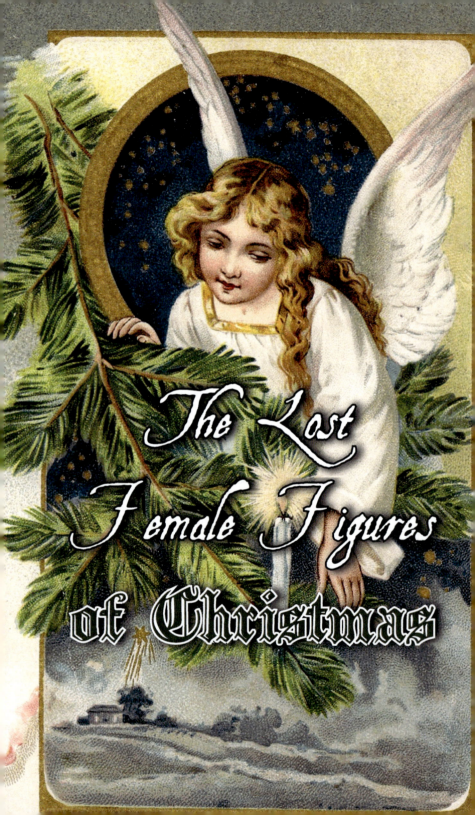

Chapter Contents

Introduction and Background	84
Modraniht: Mothers Night	85
The Important Roles of Germanic	86
Obstacles in Getting to Our Roots	88
Saint Lucia	90
Germany's Christkind	92
Snegurochka: Snow Girl	93
Holle: Bride of Wotan	95
Perchta: Demonized Goddess	97
Conversion Demonized European Figures	99
La Befana: Italy's Christmas Witch	101
Good Witches	102
Grýla: Iceland's Christmas Witch	104

Introduction & Background

It may come as a surprise that there were a great many female figures associated with the winter holiday season that have been obscured from much of our contemporary memory. Many of these figures are still popular in their home countries. But, America has a very different historical landscape when it comes to holiday practice, and it is the American brand of Christmas that has recently been exported to non-Western parts of the world.

Much has been said about Santa Claus being an amalgam of influences, and especially about his image being based on the Germanic god Odin. But, it is important to realize that there were many other holiday figures, both male and female, that did not find their way over to our modern American Christmas celebrations. German male figures such as Krampus and Knecht Ruprecht are coming up more and more in news and entertainment media. So I would like to take this opportunity to celebrate the female presence of Old Yule.

Mōdraniht: Mothers Night

A great place to start is the Anglo-Saxon holiday of *Mōdraniht*. This holiday was part of the Yule festivities. Many people already know that the "Twelve Days of Christmas" refers to the fact that Yule was not just a one day celebration, but rather a festival that lasted for several days before and after the Winter Solstice.

Mōdraniht is literally translated as Mothers Night, or Night of the Mothers. We don't know a lot about this celebration because it would have been suppressed after conversion to the more misogynist Christianity. We do know that it was a time to celebrate motherhood and probably other female ancestors (called the *Disir* by the Norse, and related to Norse *Disablot*, which was held earlier in the year). This celebration of the feminine may be related to the age old correlation between the fertility of women with fertility of crops and with rebirth of new life. The Winter Solstice, after all, celebrated the rebirth of the Sun and lengthening of days.

Just as it is in other indigenous religions, ancestor veneration was a very important aspect of Germanic spirituality. Both male and female ancestors were honored. But, female ancestors played an important role as guardians of the family line.

Hervor, daughter of Heidrek, dying at the Battle of the Goths and Huns, a painting by Peter Nicolai Arbo

The Important Roles of Germanic Women

Perhaps this has something to do with the fact that women were often the ones home guarding the homestead while men were off at war, raiding, or trading. We do know that like the Celts, Germanic women were often trained to wield a sword. Although women on the battlefield was not as common as men, it was not uncommon either. There are accounts of female bravery in battle, and it is known that certain battle tactics were designed specifically for the shield maidens. So, it might be that the women who tended the homestead were seen as strong protectresses by their children. Indeed, many Germanic female names have elements of strength and battle in them. For example, the name Mathilde translates as "mighty battle maiden."

Whatever the case may be, we know that female ancestors remained a prominent element in Germanic heathen religion. They were celebrated not only during Mōdraniht, but they also enjoyed another holiday during the Autumnal Equinox - Dísablót. While Mōdraniht is attested in Anglo-Saxon sources, Dísablót is attested in the Norse. However, both cultures share a linguistic and cultural heritage.

Also, votive inscriptions along the Rhine demonstrate that a cult of "the Mothers" (also called Matres and Matrones) existed in southern Germany, Gaul, and Northern Italy. Half of the inscriptions are Germanic, while the other half are Celtic. This again demonstrates that the Old Religion placed a high emphasis on celebrating maternity and the feminine.

Mōdraniht was celebrated on the date that we now call Christmas Eve. So this year, raise a glass and toast to your own mother, grandmother, aunts, great-aunts, and all the women who have helped raise you and yours. This is surely an old custom that can be appreciated by people of any religion today!

Lagertha, by Morris Meredith Williams, 1913

Obstacles in Getting to Our Roots

There are many aspects of folklore, tradition, and folk custom that have very deep roots. We must remember that some traditions have been immersed in Christian practice for many years, but their true origins exist in the dark crevices of old heathen custom.

The origin of such practices can be difficult to identify for a variety of reasons. The pre-Christian cultures in Northern Europe passed on their wisdom, histories, poetry, and myths orally. So in most cases, they didn't leave written records - or if they did, they either did not survive due to damp northern climabe, or were destroyed by the Church in order to propagandize history.

Another major obstacle is the way that the Catholic Church absorbed paganism, at the same time re-branding and replacing specific customs and figures. Gods became saints, pagan holidays became Christian ones. This comes as no shock to most readers. Most Christians are well aware that Christ was not born in December, that Easter is named for the pagan fertility festival in honor of the goddess *Eostre,* and so forth. It is commonly known that the Catholic cult of saints arose to turn people away from local deities.

Any student of Medieval history should be familiar with a genre of literature known as "hagiography." This is the writing of the lives of saints. Now, this genre differs greatly from biography or history because hagiographers had no intent to portray the truth in their writings. Medieval studies students are told to read hagiographical texts with a grain of salt because their purpose had more to do with an agenda than any goal of portraying the truth. The agenda being to build new figures of veneration to replace the old pagan gods and goddesses.

Now, this is not to say that all saints are bogus. But when it comes to early medieval examples, if there is not a shred of evidence outside of the hagiographical text, if the saint is closely associated with a holiday or deity, then the story of the saint should be considered nothing better than a folktale invented to replace earlier folktales, and a new religious figure invented to replace an previous one. Sometimes the stories are a mixture of fact and fiction. And, sometimes a true historical person's story could be grafted over a pagan legend creating an amalgamous figure (like Saint Brigid).

An important Northern European Goddess, most likely related to Frigga or Holle, was supplanted by the Catholic "Saint Lucia." She became popular in Sweden, but always represented as a fair Nordic woman (despite the supposed saint's origins in the Mediterranean).

Saint Lucia

Saint Lucy is an example of a widely traveled saint. She originated in the Mediterranean and is still celebrated in certain parts of that region. But, she was greatly embraced in Scandinavia where she is known as Saint Lucia. Whether or not this saint existed as a true person, I cannot say. However, whether she did or not is irrelevant to her role in Northern Europe. Saint Lucia clearly became a new entity in Scandinavia, separate and apart from what she had been in Southern Europe as her figure merged with a pre-existing Northern solstice figure.

In both parts of Europe, Lucia was, and still is, associated with light. So, that her holiday is celebrated on December 13th is significant. This strengthens Saint Lucy's ties with pagan customs. Saint Lucy's Day is one of the early mid-Winter celebrations that mark the coming of the Winter Solstice. In indigenous European religions, the Solstice marked the rebirth of the Sun. It was the end of nights becoming longer and welcoming the start of them getting shorter. Celebrating light was a common theme at this time.

In Scandinavia, there are other symbolic elements that connect Lucia to pagan times. She is often depicted carrying sheaths of grain which is a common symbol of pagan agrarian deities (also hinting at a tie to Norse Freyja). Another feature is that she is sometimes accompanied by young boys called *stjärngossar* (star boys) or *tomtenissar*. This is significant because the words "tomte" and "nissar" both describe Scandinavian elves. Elves are a prominent feature in old Germanic religion, but are not found in the Hebrew Bible.

Saint Lucia by Jenny Nystrom

Germany's Christkind

    A similar figure is Germany's *Christkind*. Unlike Lucia, she is not representative of any saint. However, what she represents is even more fascinating. Literally translated, Christkind means "Christ Child." How curious that the Christ Child is represented by a grown woman!

    The Christkind is often the one who delivers gifts to children for the Christmas holiday, as well as Saint Nicholas (who is a separate figure from Santa Claus in Germany). The fact that Germany, who's heritage shares much with that of Scandinavia, maintains a beautiful and otherworldly female figure with such a pronounced presence during Christmas celebrations is yet more evidence that the feminine was every bit as significant to our ancestors' Yuletide celebrations as male figures are at Christmas today.

Her name is "Christ-Child. But she is an adult female goddess figure

Snegurochka: Russian Snow Girl

Although most of this composition has addressed Germanic figures associated with Yule, it should be said that Celtic, Germanic, Slavic, Baltic, and Finno-Ugric cultures shared many similarity of customs and belief in the past. There are distinct differences, but they share a common Indo-European background (barring the Finno-Ugric speakers who are not IE, but still share similarities). So their languages and mythos share a common root, and similar climate and topography also makes these cultures very much alike. There is often a blending of tradition between these cultures, especially where they neighbor one another.

On that note, I introduce you to *Snegurochka*, a Russian Christmas figure. Usually translated to 'Snow Girl' in English, she is another Christmas character with complicated origins. Snegurochka is generally considered to have roots in the old Slavic pagan past. It is possible that she was once a patron goddess of winter like the Norse goddess Skaði. (And, indeed, the word Russia stems from the Norsemen who settled in the area - the Rus).

Snow Maiden, by Victor Vasnetsov, 1899

Like many European goddesses, Snegurochka lived on in the folklore of her people, even after they were converted to Christianity. Often goddesses were diminished into fairy creatures, fairy godmothers, etc. The late 19th century saw a great revival of folklore all over Europe. The most famous folklorists of this period are the Brothers Grimm. Just as they collected folktales from all over the German speaking world, Russian folklorist Alexander Afanasyev preserved the tales of his own people, thus documenting that the pre-Christian figure Snegurochka lived on during Christian times.

Religion was banned in Russia during the Soviet era. However, celebrating Russian history, and especially the history of the people (peasants), was encouraged. So, an old god of winter who had been remembered in folklore as a wizard was reinvented as the Russian version of Santa Claus - *Ded Moroz*. However, unlike the American Santa Claus, Ded Moroz travels with a lovely female companion... his granddaughter, Snegurochka.

A modern Snow Maiden and Ded Moroz in costume.

Holle:
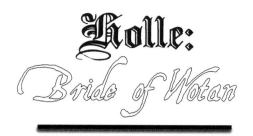
Bride of Wotan

Frau Holle is an enigmatic figure, too complicated to fully explore in this short piece. It should be noted that she maintains many similarities with other European goddesses, as well as those mentioned here. It is thought that she was once an important deity who was probably attacked and demonized by the Church in attempt to break her huge spiritual importance to the German people.

Like Snegurochka, Holle lived on in folk legend. Her tales were recorded by the Grimm brothers. They found her stories to be widespread all across the German speaking parts of Europe. Her tales exist in the Netherlands, Austria, Switzerland, the Alsatian region of France, Poland, and even into the Czech Republic.

Also like Snegurochka, Holle is associated with a powerful pagan god, Wotan. In Scandinavia, where he is known as Odin, Wotan is married to Frigga. However, in Germany, it is Holle who wears this crown. The pair ride together as they lead the infamous Wild Hunt. The Wild Hunt was a myth known throughout Northern Europe. It consisted of a host of other worldly night riders traversing the skies in a terrifying chase.

As mentioned above, it has been said that Santa Claus is at least partially influenced by Odin. Just as Santa rides through the sky each Christmas Eve, Odin rode through the night skies with the Wild Hunt during Yuletide. Unlike Santa, however, Odin brings a woman. And, sometimes, Holle was known to lead the hunt herself, without him.

The Wild Hunt, led by women, by Peter Nicolai Arbo, 1872

Perchta
Demonized Goddess

Like so many of the figures discussed before, Perchta is multifaceted. She is considered to be related to, or even another form of the goddess Holle. Perchta is known all around the German speaking world and neighboring areas. She is sometimes seen as a beautiful lady in white, and sometimes seen as a hideous monster.

Perchta also goes by many names. As Holle she is also known as Holda, Hulda. Perchta is sometimes called Berchta, Bertha, and many other variants. We mentioned that Holle is such an enigmatic figure that she can't be explained well by a short summary. But, for our purposes here, it should be said that Holle/Perchta appears to have been very wide-spread and greatly honored by the Germanic people of the continent. And, as such, a large scale campaign to halt her veneration was launched by the Church (not unlike Ostara and the campaign against her that still rages today).

Perchten monsters found throughout Alpine regions at Yuletide

While goddess Holle lived on in folklore as Frau Holle, Perchta lived on as a hideous monster who comes out of the forest to terrorize villagers at Christmas.

An old drawing of Perchta as White Goddess

Conversion Demonized
European Figures

It should be noted that the Germans of the continent were converted by and large by force. Charlemagne made it his mission to unite the Germanic tribes under one banner. But, it is easier to unite a people if they worship only one God, one system of belief. During this campaign, Germanic indigenous culture was attacked with vigor. Ancient holy trees in sacred groves were chopped down, and pagan holidays and holy figures were banned.

Because of this history, it is difficult to know if Perchta would have had both of these faces in her original context. We know that pre-Christian supernatural beings were often twisted into demonic creatures by the Church. It may come as a surprise to some to learn that creatures we view as cute and harmless, such as fairies and elves, met the same fate. Fairies became strongly associated with witchcraft and were often a key feature of witch trials.

In any case, the hideous Perchten creatures come out each year around Christmas and New Years to harass and frighten the good people who dwell in the Alps. The Perchten typically parade with another "demon" of Christmas known as Krampus, and are similar in appearance.

Vintage German holiday card featuring Krampus terrorizing children

La Befana
Italy's Christmas Witch

From Christmas demons to a Christmas witch! Children in Italy have little use for Santa Claus, it's *La Befana* who brings joy and presents. Befana is said to have a possible connection to Perchta. In fact, Northern Italy features holiday creatures very similar to the Alpine Perchten, especially where Italy borders the Alps.

There are other connections as well. Perchta/Holle is thought to be related to the *Witte Wieven*. As mentioned above, the goddess Perchta was sometimes a lady dressed in white. The Witte Wieven are feminine spirits related to the "white women" of European folklore. These women and similar ones were known all around Europe in pre-Christian times, and are still a part of Dutch folklore today. It is thought that the origins Witte Wieven stem from the veneration of the spirits of dead wise women. And, as we know, the word "witch" comes from the Anglo-Saxon word "wicce" meaning exactly that. It is not wrong to suppose that Befana, Holle, and even the Russian Baba Yaga, Celtic Cailleach, and others, are all aspects of a great pan-European goddess who was demonized as beastly monsters or "witches."

La Befana bringing gifts to Italian children

Good Witches

Witches remained very common in folklore all around Europe. Today we are most familiar with the demonized versions, the evil old hags. But, there were benevolent witches as well. La Befana is a great example of this. Good witches remained common in German folklore as well. To this day kitchen witches are found hanging on the walls of the kitchens of German women. Further, witches enjoyed their own holiday in Germany known as *Walpurgisnacht,* Night of the Witches, which takes place in the Spring on the holiday the English call "May Day" and the Celts called "Beltane."

Italy has its own history of traditional witchcraft as well. *The Benandanti* were a group of witches, both men and women, who met in secret during the 16th and 17th centuries. When questioned, they admitted to going into trance to meet up with the souls of other witches to do battle against the forces of evil. Their purpose was to protect the crops from unseen malevolent forces.

La Vecchia Religione is Italian for "the Old Religion." It said by some to have survived underground in secret all of these years. Indeed, many Italians and Italian-Americans have had a superstitious grandmother who warned against such things as "the evil eye." The Old Religion in the Italian tradition is being revived today under the name *Stregheria.*

Befana the Christmas Witch, along with the many old Italian superstitious beliefs which remain prevalent today, demonstrate that, even in seat of the Catholic Church, old beliefs die hard.

Witches illustrating a medieval French manuscript. The witch loomed large in European consciousness and is found in the imagery of many European holidays. The German May Day is associated with witches. Easter in Sweden sees little girls dressed up as witches going door to door, not unlike the Celtic Halloween as it lived on in America.

Grýla: Icelandic Christmas Witch

Another witchy figure associated with Christmas is *Grýla* - an Icelandic giantess. Although she was not known to be part of Christmas festivities until the 17th century, Grýla enjoys a long history of tradition among Icelanders. She mentioned by Snorri Sturluson in the "Poetic Edda," so she was possibly known to the Norse of previous eras as well.

In Icelandic tradition, Grýla is the mother of the Yule Lads, a group of mischievous gnomish creatures who descend from their mountain to wreak havoc in the towns below.

Grýla plays the role of the punisher of naughty children. Just as Krampus in Germany drags away bad children, Icelandic children who do not behave themselves may find themselves being carried away by the wicked Grýla.

While Norse lore does have a tradition of giants and trolls going back to pre-Christian mythos, there also is a trend found commonly across Europe where figures who were once gods and goddesses were later demonized in the post-conversion folklore. It is possible that Gryla is a figure with elements of both influences.

In this vintage illustration of Gyrla, note that she has the cloven hoofed feet, like Krampus.

The two faces of Perchta - showing a former goddess now rendered as demon

Chapter Contents

Introduction	108
Misrepresentations of European Heritage	109
The Living European Folk-Soul	112
The Yuletide Spirit	116
Bibliography and Further Reading	122

INTRODUCTION

Many Westerners have been conscious of the "war on Christmas" for several years now, and rightly so. However, years of study and deep thought has led me to completely different conclusions than most. It must be recognized, if we're honest, that our Winter Solstice holiday has been attacked before. In fact, it has been almost without regular assault for the past 1,600 years. And, while the details of this story are enough to upset a reader who cares deeply about our ancestral culture, ultimately, this is a story about the survival of spirit.

Misrepresentations of European Heritage

If we are going to behave as Aryans, that is, with honor and integrity, we must always look at history honestly and aim for truth. If we do not accept the mistruths told about our heritage by those with an agenda today, logically it follows that the same objection should be given to factions which have misrepresented and agendized European history in the past. We cannot be honest about our holiday traditions if we place them within the lexicon of a religion that originated in the Middle East and fomented in the Mediterranean. Of course there was a merger and melding over time; but in the process, a propagandized version of history was canonized.

It must be pointed out that the notion that "we" have been Christian for 2,000 years is nothing short of propaganda. The Roman Emperor Constantine converted in the 4th century A.D. That is roughly 1,700 years from today. Okay, so we're rounding up. The problem with that is that Christianity was an inherently Middle Eastern and Mediterranean religion for the first several hundred years. It spread through Britain but then retreated again when the Romans abandoned Britain at the end of the 4th century A.D. Therefore it is fair to say that Christianity was present in Britain with the Romans, but it is dishonest to say that Britain was definitively Christian. We know that Roman and Celtic native faiths were practiced in Roman Britain, as well as heretical forms of Christianity, like Gnosticism. So to assert that Britain was "Christian" under Rome is a blatant fabrication.

The Anglo-Saxons were not nominally converted

Epona is a Celtic deity who was popular in the hybrid "Gallo-Roman" religion, which was a merger of Roman and Celtic Native Faith. This figure is from Roman-occupied Germany, 2nd Century, A.D.

until the early 7th century. So now we're down from 2,000 to 1,400 years. From then on, Europe was converted by piecemeal which took centuries to another millennia. The Norse were not converted until the 10th century, the Balts not until the 14th century! In the case of Lithuania the "2,000 years" has been whittled away to 600 years. But we can keep going. The Saami in Scandinavia were still being converted as recently as the 19th century. And, it is recorded that ethnologists found rural Russian peasants in the early 20th century who had never heard of Jesus Christ. Indeed, one can search online for videos and articles on the "Mari" people of rural Russia who maintain an unbroken Native Faith until this day, often called "Europe's last pagans."

More importantly, any scholar who studies folk belief will explain quite well that the date of conversion recorded in history was a "nominal conversion." That means it was a political action made by the ruling elite to secure alliances but not embraced by the vast majority of the common people. In fact, subsequent history is quite clear that the authorities engaged in a nearly never ending cultural war against indigenous European practices from point of conversion into the Early Modern Era. Scholars call the religion of the people "popular religion," which is never in line with the religion at the top of the hierarchy. It is a continuation of their Native Faith with enough terminology superimposed over it to allow it to survive under the new religious authority.

    If we aim to tell the truth about history and look at agendas that misrepresent European cultural heritage now, then we must also be honest about the past. Just as liberals make vast sweeping statements demonizing "old white men" today, or how Hollywood shines a spotlight on African enslavement while they are silent about Europeans enslaved by Muslims, our own native history has been misrepresented. Certain phrases have been repeated so frequently that they are taken as truth when they are not true – such as the notion that "we have been Christian for 2,000 years." This is not to insult or delegitimize the faith of Christians. Rather, certain points to follow cannot be understood unless we confront common mistruths right out of the gate. There is also a fair point that Europeans have been trained to accept the disparagement of our own culture well before the current modern onslaught began.

The Baltic Pagan Temple of Romuva, in Old Prussia, destroyed in the 14th century

The Living European Folk-Soul

Another mistruth that is commonly perpetuated is that Europeans have been disconnected from their native faith for millennia. European readers will be more aware of elements of native European faith that lived on in the folk tradition than ethnic-Europeans residing in the former colonies due to the prevalence of age old customs that are still practiced throughout Europe today. That said, the holidays that we New World Europeans brought with us to new lands carried with them strong memories of our indigenous culture that was still living on in the Old World.

This is a topic that could fill a lengthy book on its own, so it is an injustice to summarize it succinctly. But, the gist of it is that once one starts poking about in the European folk tradition, which includes folklore, seasonal customs, agricultural festivals, and so on, one finds that our ancient core spirit lived on in very tangible ways. Often, our Native Faith is hiding in plain sight, but we simply lack the ability to see. Worse yet, because of the repetition of messaging such as "we have been Christian for 2,000 years" and "paganism is a dead religion," we have been collectively trained not to see what is plainly there.

Through my own studies, especially a research journey into European fairy tales, I have come to theories and conclusions that run very deeply into the intersections between psychology, language, culture, ethnicity and faith. Every human culture during the vast development of humanity on earth always maintained a holistic view of self, wherein culture, ethnicity, and mythos (faith) were one intrinsic whole before the introduction of revealed mono-theism. Science has demonstrated that neurological imprints are made on the brain by life experiences which are then passed on through DNA to offspring. If we know that genetic memory is real, one fails to see how thousands of years of cohesive culture, including language and mythos, would not leave an imprint on the shaping of the human mind. Granted, language is not a static thing, it does evolve over time. But, it is usually a slow evolution. If language and cultural experience were leaving imprints upon the minds of the people who lived for eons within their ethno-cultural group, linguistic pattern imprints would be present despite the slow evolution of language over time. This ties in to Carl Jung's theories on archetypes and the collective unconscious.

The assertion that our ancient mythos lived on in a living tradition can be seen quite readily in visually obvious ways it presents, such as the overt paganistic imagery that we still revel in at every European holiday. While our own indigenous holidays were rebranded with new Christian meanings, we did not allow our folkways to disappear. We went along with the religious authorities while carrying on the imagery, stories, symbols, and traditions that were ours for time immemorial.

Image from "Twas the Night Before Christmas" by Clement Moore illustrated by Jessie Willcox Smith, 1912

Our Folk-Soul lives on more subtly in language and linguistics. Through studying the folk tradition, I have found that linguistic clues are rife right along embedded within our folk tradition like bread crumbs. For instance, a fairy tale from in the Brothers Grimm collection, "The Star Money," makes reference to "the Good God." I had assumed that this was a Christian reference that demonstrated the melding of Christianity and indigenous European culture, and said so in my short booklet on the story. But, the phrase kept standing out to me as not ringing Christian. "The Good God" is the wording used, but there were no other Christian or biblical references, and no mention of Jesus Christ. I knew I had heard it before, so I began searching through European mythological traditions that are closely related to Germanic culture, which is my focus. Soon enough, I was reminded that the Irish god called "The Dagda" is literally translated as "the Good God."

This example can be dismissed as a coincidence by the skeptic. But, this study of fairy tales had very clearly shown other examples of overt memories of indigenous European deities that lived on in powerful ways in the European fairy tale canon ("The Three Heads of the Well" and "The Three Golden Hairs" are two other books in the series for more exploration). It goes beyond the memory of deity, though. Imagery, symbolism, our very native worldview are preserved in these tales in profound ways. Learning to see with new eyes that are able understand the imagery that is hiding in plain sight can open a whole new world of our own indigenous spirituality – which enables us to better understand ourselves and our traditions.

The crucial point is that while we might have been blinded to the understanding of our native faith, and while we may not have been conscious to its survival… as Jung might say, our conscious understanding is not really the important part of this. It lived on in our unconscious, collectively. We continued to tell tales that preserved deeply important elements of our view of the cosmos. Archetypes appeared over and over again in our stories, our holiday lore, and they still appear in our modern storytelling tradition. Aspects of our indigenous culture were ingrained permanently into our culture, but more importantly, were embedded in our very psyches.

The Germanic God, Freyr, Lord, by Johannes Gehrts, 1901

THE YULETIDE Spirit

We could fill chapters on our modern Christmas imagery that survives from ancient European tradition. But, most readers will be aware of this already. We know that decorated trees, late night gift-bringing spirits, flying animals, and elves have nothing remotely to do with the Hebrew Bible. So, there is no reason to harp in detail. But something that bears consideration that we don't stop to think about is the notion of a "Spirit of Christmas."

The phrase is usually used to denote the "feeling" of the season, of joy and encouraging kindness. But, what if there is a literal spirit of Yuletide? Whether you believe in spirits as conscious entities or merely an archetypal image that pervades our cultural unconscious and thus reappears time and time again in our cultural creations is up to the reader. Either interpretation works for our purposes here.

While "Santa Claus" as we know him is a character who really solidified in the United States in the last century, he is based on very ancient predecessors. There are a myriad of Christmastide characters who act as gift-bringers in the lore of Europe. They vary widely and may be women as well as men. Study of European mythos has caused me to shake off the pedantic view that history and mythos must be viewed linearly, orderly, chronologically, etc. Whether we're speaking of a conscious entity or of an archetype who exists in the unconsciousness of a unified Folk group, the figure is wont to shift, blend, and blur. One figure may split into two, two may merge into one. Sometimes a figure may reappear in different aspects or by different names. So therefore, that

Santa Claus appears in newer incarnation in recent American culture in no way detracts from the same entity's presence in other guises in previous eras and related cultures.

We need more time to go through the many incarnations of this figure, and a discussion of his relationship to Odin would be apt if space allowed. For now it is more important to understand the foundations of this supposition and the conditions under which this notion is theoretically possible. Thus, we have disproven the myth of 2,000 years of a monolithically Christian Europe, addressed the fallacy that European Native Faith ceased to exist, and

Old Christmas (English) riding a Yule goat by Robert Seymour, 1836

discussed how it lived on in ways that kept it hidden in plain sight. It should be briefly mentioned that the lazy history churned out by sources like the History Channel are wrong to attribute Santa Claus' origins to a Turkish saint. Certainly the name "Saint Nicholas" (which Santa Claus is a variant of) is tied to this Catholic saint. However, most readers will already be aware of the Church's tactic of superimposing saints over European deities. So, we do not need to harp on the fact that this was done. However, it is important to note that the very act of placing a Catholic saint over this figure is, in and of itself, evidence that the Church was attempting to supplant an important religious figure in the consciousness of the European people.

    Returning to the discussion of "the Good God" will help illustrate how language can be a key to decode that which has been with us all along. In my search for the reference of "the Good God," I found more than the Irish Dagda. The Dagda is often compared to the Teutonic deity called Freyr (also called Ing). They both have fertility connotations and were chief figures of their pantheons before they were displaced by incoming groups (within their mythos). Freyr's name literally means "Lord." He is the brother of Freyja, which means "Lady." "Lord" is a Germanic word. It comes from an archaic origin that means "loaf-ward," which has two meanings. The "loaf" part is a reference to grain. It can refer to the chieftain of the tribe whose responsibility it was to protect the resources of his people and ensure their prosperity, or it also refers to the deity associated with agricultural fertility – such as Freyr and the Dagda. When we know that "the Dagda" literally means "the Good God," and Freyr's name literally means "Lord," suddenly the English phrases "Good Lord" and "Good God" as exclamations have an added layer of meaning. Our very language, even as it evolved, held clues and meanings from our deep ancestral roots.

Learning to see what has been here all along is much like having blinders lifted. Suddenly we can see revelations in things we have always known but yet been blind to their depth. The discussion on genetic memory, neurological imprints passed on through DNA, and survival of our indigenous myths in our cultural unconscious can allow us to look more deeply at our own practices. For instance, how many parents of European heritage will tell their children that Santa Claus is "real" this Christmas? How many families will watch films where the central theme is that Santa's existence is called into question but he is proven to be real in the end? Why is this so important to us as a culture? If our ancient indigenous faith has long been dead, why is it so important to tell our children that this supernatural figure is real each year? Why do we get so impassioned about it? Could it be that we are unconsciously enacting beliefs that are as old as the very European consciousness itself?

Circling back to the importance of language in understanding how our ancestral mythos continues to live on in guises, we must look again at the word "Lord." As mentioned, this is a Germanic origin word that is directly

Illustration from "King Winter" by Gustav W. Seitz, published in Hamburg Germany , 1859

related to the guardian of agricultural prosperity. How, then, did it come to be used as the title for Jesus Christ? It is not a direct translation from the Greek. And, it certainly would not have been what the followers of Jesus called him, as they were Aramaic speakers. The word Lord was first ever used to refer to Christ in the Gothic Bible – a version translated to convert the Germanic Gothic tribes in the 4th Century. Who did these Goths worship as their chief deity? Ing/Freyr whose name meant Lord.

When we begin to peel back the layers of time, look into our mythos, into our very language in a deeper way, we see that so much is not as it seems. Every English speaking Christian (English being a Germanic language) who prays to "the Lord" is using wordage that denoted our own European god, OUR Lord, Freyr. Jesus' followers never called him that. When we cry out in exclamation "Good God!" or "Good Lord!" we are crying out the literal meaning of the chief deities of the Celts and Germans. Could it also be that when we speak every year of "the Christmas spirit" that we are actually speaking of a guardian entity of Yuletide? Is this why it is so very important to keep him alive in our culture?

Image from "A visit from Saint Nick" by Clement Moore, illustrated by F.O.C. Darley, 1862

Yuletide is the most sacred holiday for ethnic-Europeans and has been since pre-history. Attempts to place desert scenes of foreign characters in ethnic-costumes never worn by Europeans could not kill off our own spiritual figures who bring gifts to our children on the most sacred night of our calendar year. Attempts to attribute our Yuletide Spirit with origins as a Turkish saint could not stop him from being depicted with Northern European imagery. In short, try as they might to suppress it, the heart of our own Folk-Soul continued to beat. Essentially, it does not matter whether you believe any of this or not, for our European Folk-Soul lives on whether or not we are aware of it.

But, as for me, I believe in the Yuletide Spirit. And I believe that if our people's Folk-Soul could beat steadily during centuries of cultural oppression, that we certainly have the ability to overcome the assault we are under today. The Good God, our Lord, has been with us right along even when we were looking but not seeing. And, the Yuletide Spirit ascends on us this Winter Solstice just as he has since the birth of the European people. He has never failed to come, even when we failed to acknowledge him.

Bibliography and Further Reading:

Baker, Margaret. Discovering Christmas Customs and Folklore. Buckhamshire: Shire Publications, 1999.

Bates, Brian. The Real Middle Earth. Oxford: Sidgwick& Jackson, 2002.

Coffin, Tristram P. The Book of Christmas Folklore. New York: The Seabury Press, 1973.

Davidson, H. R. Ellis. Gods and Myths of Northern Europe. London: Penguin, 1990.

—. Myths and Symbols in Pagan Europe. Syracuse: Syracuse University Press, 1988.

Ellis, Peter Berresford. The Dictionary of Celtic Myth. London: Oxford University Press, 1992.

Emerick, Carolyn. "The Hidden History of Christmas Carols." Celtic Guide (2013): 15-19.

Fletcher, Richard. The Barbarian Conversion: From Paganism to Christianity. Berkeley: University of California Press, 1997.

Hayden, Brian. Shamans, Sorcerers, and Saints: A Prehistory of Religion. . Smithsonian Institution, 2003.

Ivanits, Linda J. Russian Folk Belief. Armonk: M. E. Sharp, Inc., 1989.

Jung, Carl. Man and His Symbols. London: Dell Publishing Co., Inc, 1968.

Lindahl, Carl, John McNamara and John Lindow. Medieval Folklore. Oxford: Oxford University Press, 2002.

MacKillop, James. Oxford Dictionary of Celtic Mythology. Oxford: Oxford University Press, 1998.

Simpson, Jacqueline. European Mythology. London: The Hamlyn Publishing Group, 1987.

Tatar, Maria, ed. The Annotated Brothers Grimm. New York: Norton & Company, Inc, 2004.

Various. Grimm's Fairy Tales. Ed. Frances Jenkins Olcott. Philadelphia: The Penn Publishing Company, 1927.

Illustration by Victor C. Anderson 1908

About the Author:

Carolyn Emerick writes about the history, mythology, and folk belief of Northwestern Europe. She has a bachelor's degree in English literature, and possesses a lifelong learning and love of European cultural heritage.

Learn more at:

www.CarolynEmerick.com

Subscribe to digital content at:

www.Patreon.com/CarolynEmerick

or

www.makersupport.com/CarolynEmerick

Follow on Facebook at

www.Facebook.com/CarolynEmerick.writer

Made in the USA
Coppell, TX
17 December 2019